to

from

THE FOLKLORE
of
LOVE
and
COURTSHIP

THE
Charms AND *Divinations*
Superstitions AND *Beliefs*
Signs AND *Prospects*
of LOVE
Sweet LOVE

Selected and Edited by
DUNCAN EMRICH

Illustrated by
TOMIE DE PAOLA

American Heritage Press
New York
A Subsidiary of McGraw-Hill

INTRODUCTION

All the items in this book were collected in the United States (chiefly New England, the South, and the Midwest) and eastern Canada (New Brunswick, Nova Scotia). A good half of them are inherited from the British Isles through Scotch-Irish-English settlers, while others are quite home-grown. Some are implicitly believed in, and for them there are "testimonials" attesting their worth and efficacy. Others are simply "for fun," but even with these there go a half-belief and a half-hope and a wish that love may come true. Some may seem absurd and outlandish, others beyond belief, and others as gentle and delicate as first love and Spring. All have been tried and tested again and again, and are woven into the grass-roots tradition of the land. They belong to yesterday and today, and to the young of all ages. They belong to tomorrow, and to love. —D.E.

FOR THE FAIRER SEX

New moon, true moon,
True and trusty,
Tell me who
My true love must be.

*

When you see the new moon over your **left** shoulder, recite:

New moon, true moon,
Dressed in blue,
If I should marry a man
Or he should marry me,
What in the name of love
Will his name be?

*

Say to the new moon over your **right** shoulder:

New moon, new moon, come play your part
And tell me who's my own sweetheart,
The color of his hair, the clothes he shall wear,
And on what day he shall appear.

Then dream.

When you see the moon for the first time in the New Year, look at it and say:

> *Whose table shall I spread?*
> *For whom shall I make the bed?*
> *Whose name shall I carry?*
> *And whom shall I marry?*

Then think of the one you would like to marry, and go your way. Ask some question of the first person you meet, and if the answer is "yes," you will marry your choice; if the answer is "no," you will not.

*

At the time of the new moon, take out a stocking, and as you knit, repeat:

> *This knot I knit*
> *To know the thing I know not yet,*
> *This night that I may see*
> *Who my husband is to be,*
> *How he goes and what he wears,*
> *And what he does all days and years.*

*

> *I see the moon*
> *And the moon sees me,*
> *And the moon sees somebody*
> *That I want to see.*

The most common daisy-petal or black-eyed Susan count:

> *He loves me,*
> *He loves me not,*
> *He loves me,*
> *He loves me not,*
> *He loves me . . .*

But also:

> *He loves me,*
> *He don't,*
> *He'll have me,*
> *He won't,*
> *He would if he could,*
> *But he can't.*

And to determine the time of marriage (which can also be done counting the teeth of a comb):

This year,
Next year,
Now,
Or never.

"*A common fortune in my girlhood was to place an apple seed on each of the knuckles of the right hand, first moistening the knuckles with a little saliva. A companion then 'named' the seeds, and the fingers were worked so as to move slightly. The seed that stayed on the longest bore the name of your future husband.*"

Name two apple seeds and put one on each temple. The one that sticks the longest will be your true love.

＊

Name two apple seeds and place them on the lids of the closed eyes. Wink. The first one to fall off is the name of your future husband.

When eating an apple, snap your finger against it and name it for your loved one. Count the fully grown seeds (all of the others are kisses) to find your fortune:

> *One's my love,*
> *Two's my love,*
> *Three's my heart's desire.*
> *Four I'll take and never forsake,*
> *Five I'll cast in the fire.*
> *Six he loves,*
> *Seven she loves,*
> *Eight they both love.*
> *Nine he comes,*
> *Ten he tarries,*
> *Eleven he goes,*
> *Twelve he marries.*
> *Thirteen honor,*
> *Fourteen riches,*
> *All the rest little witches.*

Some change the last lines to:

> *Thirteen they quarrel,*
> *Fourteen they part,*
> *Fifteen they die with a broken heart.*

*

Repeat the name of the boy you love while you cut open an apple, and if the apple contains twelve seeds, you will marry him.

On the last day of April, wash a handkerchief and hang it that night on a stalk of corn, or spread it over growing wheat in the field, or over a rosebush in the garden. The morning sun of May will dry it, and the initial or initials of the man you are to marry will appear in the wrinkles of the handkerchief.

On the last night of April, dust a pie plate with a thin layer of corn meal and place it in the garden. During the night a snail will come and with its tracks leave the initial of your lover. Snails may also be placed upon a slate or piece of brown paper, and the silvery trails that mark their passage will spell out the initial. Or a snail may be put in a fruit jar overnight, and by May morning the initial of your true love will be outlined in the jar. Also, on May morning itself, two or three snails may be placed upon a board and the board then placed in the sun. The tracks the snails make will spell out the initials of your sweetheart.

"An old Irishwoman said that when she was a girl she would hunt up all the snails she could find and put them in the milk house with a big pan of corn meal, to see the snails make the letters of her future husband's name in the corn meal."

✱

"If a young girl will pluck a white dogwood blossom and wear it in her bosom on May morning, the first man she meets wearing a white hat will have the first name of her future husband."

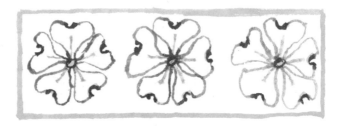

Wrap nine peas in a piece of paper upon which you have written the words "Come in, come in, my dear." Slip this piece of paper under the door mat, and the first unmarried man to enter will be your future husband.

*

When you are shelling peas and find a pod with nine peas in it, place the pod with the peas above the doorway. You will marry the first man to walk under it.

*

Over the doorway, hang a corncob from which you have shelled all but twenty kernels. You will marry the first man to enter.

*

Wear a four-leaf clover in the heel of your left shoe, and you will marry the first man you meet.

*

Place four-leaf clovers beneath the four corners of the bed sheet, and you will dream that night of your future husband.

*

If you think of a particular man while swallowing a four-leaf clover, you will marry him.

*

Hang a four-leaf clover over the doorway, and the first man to enter will become your husband.

Before going to bed at night, repeat:

> *Hoping this night my true love to see,*
> *I place my shoes in the form of a T.*

Arrange your shoes (the heel against an instep), and do not speak again that night. You will marry the man whom you see in your dreams.

*

At bedtime:

> *Point your shoes toward the street,*
> *Tie your garters around your feet,*
> *Put your stockings under your head,*
> *And you'll dream of the one you're going*
> > *to wed.*

*

On your birthday, when you go to bed at night, take off your slipper or shoe. Stand with your back to the door, and throw the shoe over your head. You must not look at it again until morning. If the toe points toward the door, you will go out of the room a bride before the year is out.

When you sleep in a strange room or bed for the first time, name the four corners of the room or of the bed for four different beaux. The first corner at which you look in the morning will give you the name of the man you will marry.

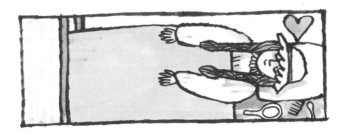

Sleep with any of the following things under your pillow, and you will dream of your true love:

> a silver spoon
> a mirror or looking glass
> a little ladder made of sticks
> a true-lover's knot of wood shavings
> a piece of wedding cake which has been
>   passed three times through a gold ring
> three pebbles which you picked up in a
>   place you had never visited before

*

Steal a salt herring from a grocery store, eat it, do not speak after eating, and the first man you dream of will marry you.

Put three raw beans in your mouth, go out of doors, stand in front of someone's window, and listen. The first man's name you hear spoken will be either that of your future husband or of the one having the same name.

*

When two girls break the wish-bone or "pulley"-bone of a chicken between them, the one getting the shortest piece will marry first, or, as the rhyme goes:

> *Shortest to marry,*
> *Longest to tarry.*

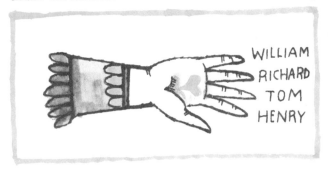

Name each of the four fingers of one hand for a different person of the opposite sex, then press or squeeze
them tightly together with the other hand. The one
that hurts the worst indicates whom you will marry.

*

If you can walk around the block with your mouth
full of water, you may be married that year.

Peel an apple without making a break in the peel and
then, after swinging it three times around your head,
throw the whole apple paring over your shoulder
onto the floor. The paring will form the initial of
your lover's name.

*

Make a string of beans, and throw it up in the air.
The initial made by the beans when they fall will be
that of the person you are going to marry.

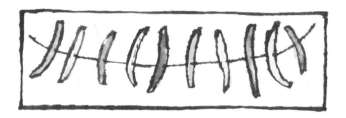

Count nine stars for nine nights. The first man you see after that will be your husband, if you care for him.

*

Count sixty white horses and one white mule, and you will marry the first man with whom you shake hands.

*

Walk seven ties of a railroad, and the first man you kiss you will marry.

*

Walk across nine cellar doors, and you will marry the first man to whom you speak.

*

The dumb, or silent, supper (which goes back to Mid-
summer Eve customs in seventeenth-century England)
must be prepared late at night, entirely in the dark;
the several girls who participate must not speak a
word during the whole affair. Everything must be
done backward: the place settings at the table are
backward, the chairs placed back to the table, the
food served walking backward from the kitchen. When
everything has been completed in utter silence and
darkness, the girls each sit, back to the table, and wait
patiently in dead silence for the stroke of midnight
and their guests. As the town clock booms out the
witching hour, the girls, staring fixedly into the black
room, will see their future husbands either walking
toward them or suddenly standing before them.

"When I was a girl, one night six of the girls I run with thought we would have a silent supper and see who would come and sit by us. Our house had one of those wide halls that went right through the house, and we girls thought we would set the table in that big hall and leave both doors open so our beaux could come in at either door. We did everything backward in the dark and did not say a word. We then set down at the table backwards to wait for our future husbands. When all at once a big storm came up and just as the clock was about to strike twelve there was a loud crash of lightning that just made the whole house tremble, and at the same time the cat and dog out in the yard had a fight and the dog ran the cat through the hall right over us. We did not know at that moment it was the dog and cat fighting. We thought it was the devil after us. Maybe you think we were not a bunch of frightened girls. We never did see our future husbands that night. We were too scared."

*

Put an egg on the fire and sit an hour. The egg will
sweat blood, and the wind will howl, the dogs will
bark, the geese will holler, and the man you are going
to marry will come in and turn the egg around. If the
egg bursts, you may never marry.

Throughout the South and Midwest (but originating in England), there is the charming custom that country girls have of going out into the woods after dark, taking hold of the tip of a leaf, and saying slowly:

If I am to marry near,
Let me hear a bird cry.
If I am to marry far,
Let me hear a cow low.
If I am to single die,
Let me hear a knocking by.

One of the sounds is always heard. Usually this is done alone, but very often two girls go together.

One woman wrote that she had done this as a young-ster with a friend and that she had heard a bird cry, but that her friend had heard a knocking. "I got married, but she never did."

*

Another version of the rhyme goes:

Low for a foreigner,
Bark for a near one,
Crow for a farmer,
Screak, tree, screak, if I'm to die first.

This must be said at midnight while walking around a peach tree.

*

Run three times around the house, and on the third round a vision of your husband will rise before you.

*

On the first day of Spring, shout into a rain barrel that stands at the corner of the house. If you hear an echo, you will marry the first unmarried man who comes around the corner of the house.

"If you want to find out your future husband, walk out of the house backward and walk to a peach tree; break off a small limb, then walk backward to the house and throw that limb in the fire; then walk backward to the door while that peach limb is burning, and when you get to the door, your future husband will grab you in his arms."

＊

Throw a ball of yarn into a barn or old house, holding the end of the yarn. Then wind it back to you, saying, "I wind, and who holds?" You will see your future husband in the barn or house.

> Stub your toe,
> Lose your beau.

On the other hand:

> Stub your toe,
> Kiss your thumb,
> See your beau
> Before evening comes.

*

If a couple are out walking together and stumble, it is a sign that they will be married.

*

If you stumble up the stairs, it is a sign of marriage. The closer to the top of the stairs, the sooner the marriage.

When a cat washes its face in front of several persons, the first person at whom it looks will be the first to be married.

Place a quilt on the floor, put a cat in the center of it, and let four or more girls take hold of the corners. Lift the quilt, and toss it and shake it to scare the cat. The girl toward whom or nearest to whom the cat jumps getting out of the quilt will be the first to be married.

*

When a girl accidentally steps on a cat's tail, she will be married within the year.

*

Before going to bed, remove seven cards from a deck without looking at them, put them in an envelope, and place the envelope under your pillow. Examine the cards the next morning. If the majority are hearts and diamonds, you will be married that year; if spades and clubs, you will not marry that year.

If a chair falls backward as you rise from it at table, you will not be married that year. If someone who wishes you ill begins to count under his or her breath before you can pick it up, the number counted stands for the number of years before you will be married.

*

Never let a man enter the front door on Monday if you want to be married. Make him come in through the back door, or you will live forever in single blessedness.

*

> *A scratch up and down*
> *Is a lover found,*
> *And a scratch across*
> *Is a lover lost.*

*

Lose your garter and you will lose your sweetheart.

*

> *Where cobwebs grow,*
> *Beaux never go!*

*

Never let anyone sweep your feet, or sweep under your feet, or sweep beneath the chair on which you are sitting—you will not marry if this happens.

*

If a skunk comes by, it is a sign of a new courtship.

*

A white pigeon coming near your doorstep means that your lover will soon propose to you.

*

The quarter in which you hear the cooing of the first dove—or the sound of the first robin—of the season is the direction from which a new sweetheart will come.

*

A white speck on your little fingernail foretells a new sweetheart.

"*Take a large rose petal, gather the edges into a ball, and hit it on your head. If it pops, he loves you. If it doesn't pop, he doesn't love you.*"

*

"*If you want to find out what boy loves you, go out in the field and get some blue thistle buds, then write the names of boy friends on paper and pin each name on the bottom of a bud. Then put them in a big pan of water and set it under your bed when you go to bed that night, and the one that loves you and you will marry will all be bloom, floating around on the top.*"

*

To know whether your sweetheart loves you, cut a lemon in half and rub both pieces on the four posts or corners of your bed, and then put the two halves under your pillow. If you see him in a dream, he is faithful. If you do not dream of him, he is faithless.

*

Think of your sweetheart when you have the hiccups. If they stop immediately, he loves you. If they continue, you are not loved by him.

When you see a turkey buzzard flying alone, say:

> *Sail, sail, lonely, lonesome turkey buzzard!*
> *Sail to the East, sail to the West,*
> *Sail to the one that I love best.*
> *Flap your wings before you fly out of sight,*
> *That I may see my true love before Saturday*
>   *night.*

If he flaps his wings three times, you will see your lover, who is true to you. If he does not flap his wings, the lover is false.

*

On Saturday night, walk around a tall white yarrow three times, saying:

> *Good evening, good evening, Mr. Yarrow,*
> *I hope I see you well tonight,*
> *And trust I'll see you at meetin' tomorrow.*

Then pluck the head, put it inside your dress, and sleep with it. The first person you meet, to speak to, at church will be your husband.

Pick a sprig of yarrow, put the stem up your nose, and say:

> *Yarrow, yarrow, if he loves me and I loves he,*
> *A drop of blood I'd wish to see.*

If blood appears, it shows that you are loved.

*

If you want to sneeze and cannot, it is a sign someone loves you, and does not dare to tell it.

*

Sneeze before breakfast, and you will see your sweetheart before Saturday night.

*

Think of the one you love when you are about to sneeze, and at the same time press your upper lip. If your beau loves you, you will not sneeze.

*

> *Sneeze before you eat,*
> *See your sweetheart before you sleep.*

If you wish to see your absent lover, the first time you go a-Maying pluck the first flower you see and breathe upon it three times, saying aloud:

> *Flower pink, flower white,*
> *I wish to see my love tonight.*

He will be sure to come.

Throw a little salt in the fire on three successive Friday nights, while saying:

> *It is not this salt I wish to burn,*
> *It is my lover's heart to turn,*
> *That he may neither rest nor happy be*
> *Until he comes and speaks to me.*

On the third Friday, he should appear.

*

If you wish your sailor lad to think of you during his absence, bury some sea sand in your pansy bed, and water the flowers before the sun shines on them.

To see your future husband in your dreams, hardboil an egg, cut it in half, discard the yolk, and fill the egg halves with salt. Then sit on something upon which you have never sat before, eat the halves, and walk to bed backwards. You will dream that your future husband comes to you carrying a cup of water. If the cup is of silver or gold, you will be wealthy; if it is of glass, moderately rich; but if it is of tin, you will be poor. And if you have the misfortune to help yourself to a drink in the dream, rather than waiting for your husband-to-be, you will not be married.

*

To determine the occupation of your future husband, grate a hazelnut, nutmeg, and walnut, and mix these with sufficient butter and sugar to make a paste. Make small pills out of the paste, and before going to bed at night swallow nine of them. If you dream of wealth, you will marry a gentleman; of white linen, a clergyman; of darkness, a lawyer; of noises, a tradesman or laborer; of thunder and lightning, a soldier or sailor; and of rain, a servant.

*

Spilling flour on the front of your dress while baking means that your husband will be a drunkard. *"I know this is so, for I never bake unless I get flour all over myself, and my husband drinks anything he can get."*

*

On St. John's Day, a maiden breaks an egg into a tumbler half filled with water at early dawn, and places it in the window where it remains untouched until sundown. At that time the broken egg is supposed to have assumed a special shape, in which the ingenious maiden sees dimly outlined the form of her future lord, or some emblem of his calling.

*

"When I was a girl, one night when the bells were ringing out the old year and the new one in, I got out of bed and got a glass one half full of water and put the white of an egg in it, and set the glass in the window. Did not say a word. Then went back to bed. In the morning when I got up, I found a perfect ship in the glass, and I married a sailor."

*

If you see a yellowbird on a holiday, you will marry a rich man.

If you see a bluebird on a holiday, you will marry a poor man.

If you see a redbird on a holiday, you will marry a sailor.

If you see a sparrow on a holiday, you will marry a man in love with a small house.

If you walk with a gentleman for the first time, and have on new shoes and go over a bridge, you will marry him.

If a gentleman and lady are riding in a carriage and are tipped out, they will be married.

If a young man rescues a girl from drowning, he will marry her.

Swallow the heart of a wild duck and you may have whom you please for a husband.

*

To win the love of a person, swallow raw a white dove's heart, point downward, and while swallowing it place your hand on the shoulder of the one in whom love is to be inspired.

*

"Here is a sure shot for an old maid to get a husband within a year. Raise a 'game rooster' to eleven months old. Kill, and draw before the body cools, cut the heart out and swallow it whole as fast as it can be removed, blood and all, and if she don't choke to death she will be married in 11 months. Our school teacher tried it & she married the janitor. She was 58 and he 61."

On Easter Monday, put on one black garter and one yellow garter, and wear them constantly, and you will have a proposal before the year is out.

*

"I had a girl friend that wanted a man she was very much in love with, and she borrowed a married woman's yellow garter and put it on her right leg and made a wish that she would get that man, and she did marry him."

A girl can win the love of any sweetheart she may desire by secretly throwing on his clothing some of the powder made by rubbing together a few heart leaves (liverwort) which have been dried before the fire. She may, if she wishes, have a score of lovers by simply carrying the leaves in her bosom.

If you want a person to love you who does not like you, make a drink of the little stout roots of lady's-tresses (Spiranthes) and give it to him, and he will immediately love you.

*

Take some amaranth seeds, some pounded wheat, the first honey from a new hive, and a white dove's heart, dried and powdered. Make these into a cake, and get your loved one to eat it if you wish to win his love.

*

A love potion made of a certain number of red and white rose leaves and forget-me-nots, boiled in 385 drops of water for the sixteenth part of an hour, will, if properly made, insure the love of the opposite sex, if three drops of the mixture are put into something the person is to drink.

*

If a girl wishes a young man to fall in love with her, she may offer him a glass of beer, cider, or lemonade, into which she has stirred a teaspoonful of her finger-nails, which have been ground into powder.

Always carry the heart of an owl, and you can get whom you want.

*

If you can walk nine ties of a railroad track without stepping off the rails, you can marry anyone you choose.

*

If you can make your forefinger and little finger touch together over the back of your two middle fingers, you can get whomever you want.

*

Pluck a feather from the tail of a rooster and put it in your glove. Then shake hands with the man you want, and you will get him.

*

You can secure anyone you want by cutting your nails on nine successive Sundays.

*

"When you meet a person at a party and you wish him or her to be your affinity, repeat their name in a low voice twenty times right there. Then that night, just before going to sleep, wish twenty times you will see them again, and you will sure get them."

*

Rub your hands in sweet fern. The first one you shake hands with afterward is your true love.

*

If a girl tucks a piece of fern or a piece of southern-wood† in the toe of her shoe, she will marry the first boy she meets.

Also, if she puts a piece of southernwood down her back, she will marry the first boy she meets. Hence the plant is called "boy's love."

*

If a marriageable woman puts a piece of southern-wood under her pillow on retiring, the first man whom she meets in the morning is the one whom she is to marry.

†southernwood: a shrubby wormwood with yellowish flowers and fragrant leaves.

*

FOR THE GENTLEMEN

You can secure a girl's love by pulling a hair from her head.

*

If you want to get married, stand on your head and chew a piece of wit leather (gristle) out of a beef neck and swallow it, and you will get any woman you want.

*

Make a love potion by drying and crushing to a powder the web of a wild gander's foot. A pinch of this in your loved one's coffee will cause her to fall in love with you and remain faithful. (Wild geese take only one mate.)

To make a young girl fall madly in love, hide the dried tongue of a turtledove somewhere in her room. She will be helpless to resist your advances.

*

To win a maiden, the lover should count her steps up to the ninth one, then take some earth from the track made by her left heel, and carry it in his pocket for nine days.

If you want to have good luck with a girl, just wear
a rose.

And, lastly and gently:

> *Dear, dear doctor,*
> *What will cure love?*
> *Nothing but the clergy,*
> *And white kid glove.*

My own collections aside, it is a pleasure to acknowledge the following sources: Fanny D. Bergen, *Current Superstitions*, Boston, 1896, and *Animal and Plant Lore*, Boston, 1899; Ray B. Browne, *Popular Beliefs and Practices from Alabama*, Berkeley, 1958; Arthur Huff Fauset, *Folklore from Nova Scotia*, New York, 1931; Harry M. Hyatt, *Folklore from Adams County, Illinois*, New York, 1935; Vance Randolph, *Ozark Superstitions*, New York, 1947; Earl J. Stout, *Folklore from Iowa*, New York, 1936; Annie Weston Whitney and Caroline Canfield Bullock, *Folklore from Maryland*, New York, 1925.